BUILDING STRONG CONNECTIONS AND RESTORING BROKEN PARENT-CHILD RELATIONSHIPS

Parenting Guide For Families

SYLVESTER WEBSTER

Table of Contents

Chapter 5
How to mend a strained bond between parents and grown children:

Introduction

Welcome to the path of developing a synergy with your kids and repairing strained bonds. This book serves as a guide for parents who want to juggle the difficulties of adolescence while reestablishing trusting and meaningful relationships with their kids. It underlines how crucial it is to create a solid foundation throughout infancy so that loving connections can endure the sensitivity of puberty.

In this book, we examine how a child's formative years prepare them for a strong parent-child relationship. We examine the value of a stable connection, good communication, trust, and respect for one another, all of which help build a strong foundation. We want to provide parents with the information and resources they need to successfully navigate the special complexity of adolescence by looking at how early training affects the parent-child connection.

Physical, emotional, and cognitive changes characterize adolescence as a formative stage. It is a period of growing independence, discovering oneself, and creating a personal identity. This era can be difficult for parents as they want to nurture and understand their adolescent children while still recognizing their need for independence.

In light of studies and observations, we highlight the importance of early education in preparing parents to maintain their bond with their kids during the turbulent adolescent years. The foundation for navigating the delicate dynamics of adolescence is laid out through good communication, emotional intelligence, setting boundaries, and modelling healthy behaviours, which is what we cover in this article.

In addition, we explore the various traps that parents should be aware of, such as oversensitivity, a lack of comprehension, and the risks of overprotectiveness. By addressing these issues, we enable parents to interact with their adolescent children in a way that fosters open communication and demonstrates empathy.

This book provides helpful guidance, tactics, and activities to help parents and their adult children mend fences, regain trust, and develop healthier relationships. We understand that every parent-child connection is different and that no one method works for all situations. As an alternative, we provide a road map for introspection, development, and the building of a strong and enduring parent-child connection.

We urge you to engage in this adventure with an open mind, an eagerness to learn, and a dedication to making progress. You may build the synergy essential to deepen the tie between parents and children and establish a connection that endures the trials of puberty and beyond by investing in your relationship with your kids and putting the concepts presented in this book into practice.

As we set out on a journey to constructing solid foundations and nurturing enduring connections, let's start this revolutionary investigation into collaborating with your kids and repairing damaged relationships.

Chapter 1

Why there is a rift between parents and children?

Before talking about how to repair a damaged parent-child connection, we need first to explore the most frequent causes of these relationships, to begin with. The teenage years are when parent-child relationships are most likely to fall apart.

Teenagers have difficulties during adolescence as they continue to grow emotionally, psychologically, and physically. When a kid enters puberty, their relationship with their parents sometimes grows distant, and parents may find themselves at a loss on how to deepen their connection with their teenagers.

A person's life goes through a substantial time of sensitivity and change during adolescence. Children go through physical, emotional, and cognitive transformations throughout this period that mould their identities and provide the groundwork for their future growth. This stage, also known as the teenage years, usually starts around the time puberty sets in and lasts until late adolescence or the beginning of early adulthood.

The increased sensitivity people go through in adolescence is one of its primary characteristics. Teenagers are more open to peer pressure and the views and judgements of others. This sensitivity results from a need to be accepted, and socially included, and carve out an identity within a wider social environment. The judgments of friends and classmates carry a lot of weight and frequently affect an adolescent's self-esteem, behaviour, and decision-making.

Individuals also go through a rise in emotional sensitivity during adolescence. Hormonal shifts can cause severe mood swings, which can be exacerbated by the difficulties of negotiating complicated social relationships and becoming adults. Adolescents may be more prone to emotional outbursts, mood swings, and heightened sensitivity to criticism or rejection. The teenage years may be a turbulent period for both adolescents and their parents or caregivers due to this emotional sensitivity.

Another component of adolescence that requires attention is cognitive sensitivity. Adolescents have substantial cognitive growth at this time, including the ability to think critically, and abstractly, and take hypothetical scenarios into account.

However, this enhanced cognitive capacity may also increase their sensitivity to contradictions, injustices, and ethical conundrums. Adolescents may challenge authority, question social conventions, and show a stronger sense of idealism and enthusiasm for social justice problems.

To help and mentor young people throughout this transforming stage, it is critical to grasp and comprehend the sensitivity of adolescence. Teenagers need a safe, accepting atmosphere where they may explore their identities, express their feelings, and make mistakes without worrying about being harshly judged or punished. Building trust, keeping lines of communication open, and offering emotional support are essential in promoting resilient growth at this delicate time.

An atmosphere that is supportive of teenagers must be created by parents, other family members, educators, and society at large. It's critical to actively listen, acknowledge their thoughts and experiences, and offer advice without being overbearing. Adolescents can better traverse the challenges of decision-making and personal development if their autonomy is respected while adults provide direction and establish limits.

Adolescents' general well-being may also be improved by encouraging good mental health behaviours, teaching emotional control techniques, and encouraging healthy relationships and social connections. Encouragement of extracurricular activities, hobbies, and involvement in the community can give them opportunities for self-expression and personal growth.

The foundation for good growth and development throughout this transitional era of life can be laid by acknowledging the sensitivity of adolescents and embracing a caring and understanding attitude. Adolescents can be empowered to overcome obstacles, form a solid sense of self, and thrive as they enter adulthood by receiving the proper support and direction.

This just serves to highlight how important parents are to how we nurture our children and how we shape their adolescent years. Parents often don't realize that they only have between 14 and 16 years to nurture and discipline their children. The main focus is on raising kids to be competent in making moral judgments while they are young.

Parents must get rid of the idea that they should be making decisions for their kids

while they are young instead of guiding them
as they mature into teenagers.

Chapter 2

The Parent's objectives for their children

Arguments between parents and teens can occur about everything from spending money to clothing and curfew. Learn about some of the issues that might cause parent-teen conflict as well as possible solutions.

When two persons have opposing aims, values, or beliefs, conflict results. It's not always as straightforward as a debate. Conflict, on the other hand, is the disagreement that takes place just before an argument breaks out and names are hurled.

There are naturally numerous occasions for confrontation between parents and teens. Since teenagers may think independently yet still reside with parents who have expectations and restrictions for them, adolescence is a time when independence and parental influence collide. Teenagers don't always share their parents' opinions and values, and their desire to have fun competes with their parents need to keep them safe.

Raising children to be independent, and capable of making the proper judgments at a young age without consulting us, should be one of the parents' primary goals. The true responsibility of parents is to develop their children to a point where we can trust their judgment, and this requires extensive modelling beginning at a young age.

We must colonize[i.e Educate]. Whether we agree with their decision or not, it's crucial to educate them to the point where we can trust that they will make wise choices throughout their life. However, how we raise kids affects their capacity to make wise choices. 99% of parent-child relationships end when the child is a teenager or young adult.

The foundation set during early education is vital in supporting kids even throughout the delicate adolescent stage; it helps them establish limits while they are still open to discovering new things. The dynamics and resiliency of a child's transition into adolescence are significantly influenced by the events, relationships, and parenting strategies throughout the early years.

An in-depth examination of how a solid foundation from early education might aid kids in navigating the difficulties of the adolescent stage:

Secure Attachment: Children that have a secure attachment during their early years feel protected, trusted, and emotionally secure. The foundation for a strong link that can weather the upheaval of adolescence is laid when parents have a loving and receptive relationship with their kids throughout the formative years. Securely attached children are more likely to seek out and maintain positive relationships with their parents when they get older. This secures their bond when the child experiences all of the new adventures of teenage age and helps parents lead their children rather than dictating or pushing their experience on the youngster.

Effective Communication: Early education that stresses these abilities paves the way for frank discussions between parents and their children. It is simpler to keep open lines of communication with adolescents when parents have created a practice of active listening, empathy, and polite communication during childhood. Teenagers are more willing to express their ideas, worries, and difficulties with their parents when they feel heard and understood, which strengthens and secures the bond between them.

Trust and Mutual Respect: A successful parent-child relationship requires both trust and mutual respect. It lays a solid basis for trust and respect to last throughout adolescence when parents constantly show that they are trustworthy, respect their child's limits, and treat them with dignity. This foundation aids parents in navigating the inherent difficulties of developing trust and establishing boundaries during the delicate adolescent time.

Emotional intelligence: Early education that emphasizes emotional intelligence gives kids the tools they need to comprehend and control their emotions. A supportive environment for emotional expression is created by parents who assist their kids in growing up with emotional awareness, empathy, and emotional control. During adolescence, when emotional intensity and instability are at their peak, this foundation is vital. Teenagers who have a solid foundation in emotional intelligence are better able to control their emotions, express their feelings, and ask their parents for help.

Setting Boundaries and Discipline: When children are being trained, effective boundary-setting and discipline provide a framework of expectations and rules.

Adolescents benefit from the protection and structure that clear, consistent limits offer as they negotiate their growing independence. It is simpler to renegotiate and modify parental limits to meet the changing requirements of adolescents when such boundaries have previously been set throughout childhood.

Providing role models for children is an important part of early education. Teenagers are more likely to imitate the behaviours of their parents if they are frequently exposed to positive behaviours, beliefs, and healthy relationships as children. Parents establish an example for teenagers to follow by demonstrating effective problem-solving, polite communication, and empathy, building a healthy and stable connection.

Maintaining Connection and Quality Time: Early childhood education that places a strong emphasis on keeping the lines of communication open and spending quality time with children paves the way for ongoing closeness throughout adolescence. The parent-child bond is strengthened when parents prioritize and set aside time for their children's interests, meaningful interactions, and shared activities. Even throughout the turbulent adolescent years, these continual ties foster a sense of belonging and emphasize the value of the relationship.

adaptation and Flexibility: Parental coping with the challenges and changes associated with adolescence is facilitated by early education that promotes adaptation and flexibility. It develops a feeling of understanding and mutual development when parents have shown the capacity to modify their parenting method, expectations, and style in response to their child's changing needs. This flexibility aids parents in managing the delicate issues and particular needs of puberty while preserving a safe and loving bond with their adolescent.

Parents may establish a stable, honest, and resilient connection with their children during adolescence by laying a solid basis for it during childhood training. At this critical stage of adolescence, the early experiences, communication styles, trust, and emotional ties developed during infancy can help secure their connection.

Chapter 3

The relationship between parents and their adolescents is impacted by parental oversensitivity.

The parent-child connection may suffer as a result of parents' excessive sensitivity to and lack of comprehension of their teens. Insensitive parents may become too invasive, overly protective, or unduly judgmental of their adolescent's decisions and behaviour. This conduct can result in difficult parent-child relationships, a lack of trust, and strained communication.

The following are some ways that excessive sensitivity and a lack of comprehension can damage the bond between parents and their children:

Lack of Independence: Very sensitive Teenagers may struggle to become independent. Parents who are too concerned and nervous all the time with their kids may unintentionally discourage them from making choices, taking chances, and growing through their own experiences. This may lead to a lack of self-assurance and a feeling of dependency on parental supervision, which may deteriorate the connection between parents and children.

Overly sensitive parents may find it difficult to successfully interact with their adolescent children. They could overreact or respond emotionally to their child's thoughts, feelings, or behaviours as a result of their ongoing anxiety and dread. Adolescents may feel criticized, misunderstood, or anxious about failing their parents as a result, which can make it difficult for them to be open and honest with one another. The parent-child connection may suffer and the growth of trust and understanding may be hampered by the absence of a secure and encouraging environment for communication.

Oversensitivity and a lack of comprehension can cause trust between parents and teenagers to be strained. Parents who are continuously doubting or criticizing their adolescent's actions are demonstrating that they do not have trust in their adolescent's capacity to make wise decisions. This lack of trust might cause the teenager to feel resentful, defiant, and secretive, further eroding the connection.

Emotional Distance: Overly sensitive parents may find it difficult to offer the understanding and support that teenagers require during this time of rapid development. Teenagers could believe that their feelings and experiences are not acknowledged or taken seriously, which could cause a sense of emotional separation between parents and kids. Feelings of loneliness and a weakened sense of belonging within the family might result from this emotional detachment.

Impact on Self-Esteem: Parents' oversensitivity can also have a detrimental effect on teenagers' sense of self-worth. Feelings of inadequacy, self-doubt, and a sense of self-worth might be brought on by relentless criticism, excessive protection, or unreasonable expectations. Adolescents may believe that their parents do not completely appreciate or understand them for who they are as people, which can strain the parent-child connection.

Teenage Age as a Cause of Conflict Between Parents and Children.

1. Curfew: Parents and teens frequently disagree over the issue of curfew. No matter what hour the curfew is, parents worry when their children don't get home when they're supposed to. An anxious parent starts to reprimand their children. When the teen does return home, they receive a harsh reprimand and an earful.

This would have been resolved when they were still infants because it is against their development to let them express their free will. Many people spend time and money teaching their pets how to behave, but we spend less time and money teaching our infants. We should have designed an easy technique to teach our child. I've recently witnessed infants as young as age[2] swimming in a pool on their own. Such a youngster can never forget how to swim, and parents should never worry about their 15-year-old boy or girl swimming in the largest pool in the world. Don't blame them if you don't train them.

2. Use of Cell Phones: From a technological standpoint, cell phones are a relatively recent cause of conflict. It is related to other sources of conflict, such as how to spend money and the proper forms of affectionate expression. The argument usually arises when adolescent uses their mobile phone extensively, either to communicate with a significant other or to build up a very large phone bill. Phones are occasionally used in improper ways, such as for sexting.

3. Noise: Parents don't appear to have the same tolerance for noise as teens, whether it comes from a party, an electric guitar, or the television. Teenagers occasionally choose loud entertainment to their parents' need for sleep. Every day, conflicts like this one come up. Conflicts over music might also fall into this category since parents are more likely to instruct their children to turn it down if they don't like the music they are listening to.

Giving them time to play while they were still infants could have prevented this, and when the time was up, the baby would learn to respect his or her parents for that and adjust. By the time such a child was a teenager, he or she would be accustomed to time management and the significance of each hour of the day.

4. When you're a teenager, there are a thousand reasons a parent could not approve

of your boyfriend or girlfriend. There are also a thousand justifications for the parent's unfairness. If their children are old enough to date at all, parents likely believe that they are too young for them to make wise decisions.

5. Church/faith: Parents may easily persuade their young children to attend church and practice their faith. However, as a youngster gets older, their thought processes get more sophisticated and abstract. Peers, professors, coaches, and the media begin to have an impact on them. Parental and teen ideas on the existence of God, who God is, and the significance of the church may differ.

6. Grades: If there is one simple, standardized way for parents to determine a teenager's maturity and level of responsibility, it is to look at their grades. Parents could still use this information to evaluate a teen each time their grades are reported, even when it may

be untrue. While some parents are uncomfortable with Fs, others refuse to see Cs. In any case, when parental expectations aren't satisfied, conflict results.

7. Fairness: While no one enjoys working for nothing, occasionally youngsters mistake completing chores for free labour. They are probably receiving something material from their parents in exchange, but the youngster might not be aware of it. For instance, parents can be giving their children access to transportation, clothing, food, and housing. That, however, is insufficient compensation when you are young and self-centred for cleaning your room and carrying out the garbage. Similar to how grades could not live up to parental expectations, allowances might not match the expectations of the teenager.

8. Personal Appearance: Parents who value conventional appearance are easy to rile up

with tattoos, piercings, wild hairstyles, heavy makeup, or short skirts. It's a little paradoxical that many teenagers desire to get a tattoo or piercing to exhibit their uniqueness while there are millions of other teenagers who do the same thing.

9. Use of drugs, alcohol, and cigarettes: No parent ever expresses a desire for their kids to use illicit drugs. Parents' hopes for a bright future for their children are dashed when they find that their adolescent is struggling with substance abuse. By the time the parents find out about it, it has probably already been a problem.

10. Dishonesty: Being honest is already a touchy subject for some individuals. Parents who are in control of their adolescent will likely feel unhappy if they find out the adolescent is lying to them directly. Typically, falsehoods are spoken to cover up

another crime, such as stealing, sneaking out, or an unsightly tattoo. Teenagers who break their parents' trust may find it challenging to escape the hole they dug for themselves.

11. Using Electricity/Hot Water: Using electricity or hot water can easily cause problems when the parents are paying for something that the child appears to use irresponsibly. Have you ever heard a phrase like "Seize the lights, shut the door, were you birthed in a barn?" Do these words ring a bell with you?

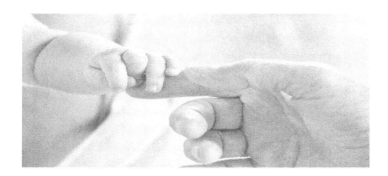

Chapter 4

How are parent-teen disputes resolved?

Finding the reason for the issue is the first step towards solving it. Parents and teens alike can benefit from the following advice:

Concentrate on your common goals: See each other as partners in attaining your shared goals, which are frequently to protect the safety and success of adolescents. Refocus your efforts on reaching these goals to prevent being unduly combative.

When stating your opinions and offering ideas, use the "I statement". Simply saying, "I feel _____ when I _____," may be used to make direct and explicit requests. This is much better than blaming others and calling them names, which commonly happens when emotions are running high.

To aid with alternate thinking, make a list of possible resolutions to the problem. This may seem obvious, yet disagreements can cause ideas to become so polarized that reaching a compromise or reaching a compromise seems impossible. Don't worry about if your initial ideas seem realistic; just start putting them down. You may use creativity to overcome any problem in life, including interpersonal ones.

conclude together. Even if parents tell their kids they have to do something "because I said so," or if the teen just gives in to pressure and the relationship suffers, there is still a conflict. Choose a course of action together after everyone is composed enough to think logically. However, refrain from attempting this while someone is furious.

To be more effective, keep your composure. Avoid making decisions while you are still upset and abstain from pointing fingers, either literally or symbolically.

Five Things to Do to Improve Parent-Teen Relationships

Adolescence presents challenges for teenagers as they continue to develop emotionally, mentally, and physically. Puberty usually causes a child's relationship with their parents to grow distant, and occasionally parents struggle with how to rekindle a tight bond with their adolescents. Even if the children are now adults, the relationship between parents and children may be coming to an end.

Teens may come out as distant, disrespectful, egocentric, and unmanageable from the perspective of their parents. They don't seem to be as talkative or gregarious as they were when they were younger, so it may be difficult to understand what drives their behaviour.

A teen perspective: Parents may come out as obtrusive and careless. Teenagers usually think that their parents don't understand them, aren't aware of their challenges, or just don't care about them. When they feel misunderstood, they lose their temper and act out.

These five simple relationship-building exercises can help parents and teens' relationships get better and stronger. Sharing adventures and quality time might improve your relationship. Numerous of these activities may be changed to accommodate the requirements of younger children.

A time when your teen is not engaged in any other activities is ideal.

The Value of Likes and Dislikes in Communication Honest communication is essential to developing a positive, healthy relationship between parents and teenagers, according to several researchers. Since it provides parents and teens with a chance to practice active listening and effective communication, this first exercise can enhance communication.

Instructions

Sit down with your teen in a place where there won't be any interruptions.

Make a list of three things you like and three things you would change about the other person on your sheet of paper.

Take this chance to promise each other that you will try your best to listen to each other's thoughts without interjecting and to pay them your whole attention when you are both finished. Additionally, agree that neither of you will act disrespectfully toward the other throughout the dialogue by becoming irate, defensive, or judgmental. Remember that the goal of this activity is to enhance communication.

Go over what each of you wrote in turn.

2. Walking while wearing blinders: Building trust

Trust is one of the key tenets of a strong interpersonal relationship. It's important to remember that trust can grow slowly or it can be rapidly shattered. Trust is a two-way street. The next activity's purpose is to foster trust.

Instructions

Make sure one individual is completely vision-impaired by blindfolding them.
Ask the individual who is not wearing the blindfold to lead the blind person about the home for 10 to 15 minutes.

Discuss how it felt to be led around the home without being able to see and to have to entirely rely on the other person afterwards.
So that the other person may experience directing or being directed, switch roles and then repeat.

3. Poetry and Memory: Appreciating Perspectives It can be difficult to talk about a recent experience, especially if it was bad, since we may not feel that the other person

understands or is listening to us completely and without bias. Examining a past occurrence or circumstance involving a parent and an adolescent is the focus of this writing assignment. The situation might either be favourable or unfavourable.

Instructions

Get some paper and pens, and take a seat somewhere peaceful. Write a six-sentence poem that expresses your feelings on a specific circumstance or incident that affects both participants without looking at each other's work.

The other person should hear you read your poetry aloud. Ask the other person to attempt to determine the circumstance that the poetry is referencing.

Talk to the other person about how you're feeling and the effect the incident has had on you.

Do this poetry practice in pairs.

4. Design: Listening Techniques
For effective interpersonal communication, supportive listening skills are crucial. Learning to listen well may improve communication, aid in dispute resolution, and provide constructive assistance to people in need. Spend some time as a parent showing your kids the qualities of attentive, encouraging listening.

Instructions

Together, take a seat on a comfy floor, back to back. For comfort, you might want to employ cushions or other supporting tools. Have one person demonstrate how to draw anything, one step at a time, with paper and pencils in hand. This may be a landscape, a face, a collection of forms, etc. After that, turn to face one another and look at each other's artwork.

Engage in dialogue about the exercise.

Note: This activity might be modified to use different materials like paint, clay, or even legos or building blocks. The workout with Jenga blocks is seen in the video above. Of sure, you are acquainted, but might you be more familiar?

5. Favorites: Learning About You

How well do parents who have teenagers know one another's likes and dislikes, even though they probably live together and communicate frequently? Parents and teenagers may learn about one other's favourite things with this writing practice.

Instructions

Find a peaceful, cozy spot to sit.

Write a list of your favourite colour, number, TV program, book, topic in school, snack, drink, friend, and activity with a pen and paper in hand, all without peeking at the work of the other person. Take turns speculating on one another's responses. Finish with a discussion of the exercise and what you each learnt from it.

Chapter 5

How to mend a strained bond between parents and grown children

It can be difficult and delicate to mend a damaged bond between parents and adult children. It takes patience, comprehension, and a readiness to consider the inadequacies and errors of the past.

Rebuilding the connection can be aided by doing the following actions:

Accept Responsibility: Both parents and adult children need to accept responsibility for the damaged relationship. This entails accepting accountability for prior behaviours, actions, and communication patterns that could have aided in the breakdown. It necessitates sincere introspection and a readiness to make apologies.

Open and Honest Communication: Restoring trust and understanding requires open and honest communication to be established. Without passing judgment, each participant should be given the chance to share their thoughts, worries, and wishes. To create a safe and fruitful environment for conversation, active listening, empathy, and non-defensive replies are essential.

Genuine sincere apologies from parents and adult children can be effective in mending previous scars. Rebuilding trust can be aided by expressing regret, admitting the harm done, and making restitution. Similarly to this, moving on and building a new foundation for the relationship depends on being able to forgive and let go of anger.

If necessary, seek professional assistance: Sometimes working with a therapist or counsellor can be helpful. A qualified expert may give direction, encourage dialogue, and offer methods for resolving disputes and addressing underlying problems. They may offer an unbiased viewpoint, aid in the process of rebuilding, and assist in navigating difficult emotions and dynamics.

Establishing healthy limits and honouring each other's individuality and autonomy are essential to mending the relationship. Parents and adult children should respect each other's limits while properly communicating their needs and expectations. It's crucial to respect individual preferences and give room for development.

Develop Empathy and Understanding: Understanding one another's viewpoints and cultivating empathy for one another helps promote compassion and close connection gaps. Rebuilding relationships and fostering empathy can be facilitated by acknowledging that each person has their own distinctive experiences, beliefs, and difficulties.

Focus on the Present and the Future: While it is vital to address the past, the relationship needs to be repaired to concentrate on the present and the future. Focus on creating pleasant memories and cultivating a better dynamic going forward rather than concentrating on regrets and frustrations from the past.

Invest Time and Effort: It takes time, consistency, and effort from both sides to mend a damaged relationship. It is a continuing commitment to development and progress rather than a fast cure. Over time, a relationship may be strengthened by spending time together frequently, making new experiences, and actively expressing love and support.

Conclusion

We aim to leave you with a renewed feeling of optimism and useful strategies to establish stronger ties with your adolescent children as we wrap up our discussion on fostering synergy with your children and mending damaged relationships. Adolescence is no exception to the parenting journey's abundance of joys, difficulties, and growth opportunities. We have discovered the essential components needed for navigating the delicate waters of adolescence by appreciating the importance of early training and the effect it has on the parent-child connection.

Laying a solid foundation when still young serves as the cornerstone of resilient parent-child interactions, as we have often stressed throughout this book. To develop a strong link that can resist the upheaval of adolescence, we have looked at the importance of secure attachment, good communication, trust, and mutual respect. We may provide an atmosphere that fosters the development, independence, and intercultural understanding by realizing the risks of oversensitivity and the need to modify our parenting strategies.

It is important to recognize that mending damaged bonds requires time, perseverance, and work from both parents and their adult children. The first stages to forging a better connection are to mend old wounds, apologize, forgive, and set appropriate limits. We have stressed the value of open and honest communication, getting professional assistance when necessary, and concentrating on the present and future rather than lingering on the past.

By making time for our relationships with our kids throughout their formative years, we provide them with the knowledge, principles, and fortitude they'll need to face adolescence's obstacles. Positive self-esteem, emotional intelligence, problem-solving skills, and self-discipline are all fostered through effective child training. Adolescents who are dealing with peer pressure, academic pressure, and the quest for personal identity can benefit greatly from these attributes.

To address the changing demands of our teenage children, we as parents must modify our strategy. By embracing their increasing independence and giving them the freedom to express themselves, we give them the capacity to make moral decisions and grow into self-assured, kind people. We exhibit our steadfast support and dedication to their well-being by staying in touch, spending quality time with them, and serving as great role models.

We would like to conclude by inviting you to begin this transforming path of developing synergy with your kids. You can restore, improve, and deepen your relationship with your adolescent children by putting the ideas and tactics covered in this book into practice. Never forget that there is always time to restore damaged relationships, treat injuries, and promote understanding. You may build a relationship with commitment, tolerance, and love that will withstand the difficulties of adolescence and serve as the cornerstone of a lasting relationship.

May you use this book as a roadmap, a springboard for inspiration, and a reminder of the transformational power of solid, caring, and safe parent-child connections. We urge you to celebrate your progress, embrace the particularity of your path, and treasure the opportunities for connection, personal development and shared experiences as you go ahead. Together, let's build enduring bonds with our kids, encouraging love, empathy, and a feeling of unity that will last us through parenting and beyond.

Printed in Great Britain
by Amazon

43782526R00036